Robert Frost

by Susan Temple Kesselring

Content Consultant
Anne Goldman
Professor of English
Sonoma State University

CORE
LIBRARY

Published by ABDO Publishing Company, PO Box 398166, Minneapolis, MN 55439. Copyright © 2013 by Abdo Consulting Group, Inc. International copyrights reserved in all countries. No part of this book may be reproduced in any form without written permission from the publisher. The Core Library™ is a trademark and logo of ABDO Publishing Company.

Printed in the United States of America,
North Mankato, Minnesota
112012
012013
♻ THIS BOOK CONTAINS AT LEAST 10% RECYCLED MATERIALS.

Editor: Kari Cornell
Series Designer: Becky Daum

Cataloging-in-Publication Data
Kesselring, Susan Temple.
 Robert Frost / Susan Temple Kesselring.
   p. cm. -- (Great American authors)
Includes bibliographical references and index.
ISBN 978-1-61783-717-3
1. Frost, Robert, 1874-1963--Juvenile literature. 2. Poets, American--19th century--Biography--Juvenile literature.   I. Title.
811/.52--dc23
[B]
                                        2012946798

Photo Credits: Marty Lederhandler/AP Images, cover, 1; AP Images, 4, 13, 33; The Washington Post/Getty Images, 6; De Agostini Picture Library/Bridgeman Art Library, 10; Library of Congress, 16, 20, 28, 30; Bettmann/Corbis/AP Images, 23, 40, 45; Jeffrey M. Frank/Shutterstock Images, 24; Red Line Editorial, 27, 39; Fotosearch/Getty Images, 35; Ken Wiedemann/iStockphoto, 36

CONTENTS

CHAPTER ONE
The Poet and the President   **4**

CHAPTER TWO
A Difficult Childhood   **10**

CHAPTER THREE
Love and Family   **16**

CHAPTER FOUR
The Poet Farmer   **24**

CHAPTER FIVE
Published in England   **30**

CHAPTER SIX
Joys and Sorrows   **36**

Important Dates..........................42
Key Works 43
Stop and Think 44
Glossary................................46
Learn More..............................47
Index 48
About the Author 48

CHAPTER ONE

The Poet and the President

The year was 1960, and American poet Robert Frost was feeling like he was on top of the world. An award called the Robert Frost Medal had been created in his honor. This award is still given to poets today. For many years, no one seemed to care about Frost's poetry. But now, at age 86, Robert Frost had the world's full attention. People loved his poems.

Robert Frost visits President John F. Kennedy at the White House on January 22, 1961, two days after Kennedy took office.

Frost takes a walk through Dumbarton Oakes Park in Washington DC with friend Stewart Udall.

Robert Frost was truly a poet of the American people. His poems used the everyday language of people in New England, where he lived. Frost believed poems were meant to be spoken aloud, so he paid close attention to the rhythm and sound of each word. Frost was able to capture perfectly in words the image of a quiet country lane. His poems often explored nature or relationships, themes that were familiar and comfortable to his readers.

An Invitation from the New President

In November 1960, John F. Kennedy was elected president of the United States. As Kennedy was getting ready for his inauguration, his friend and Interior Secretary, Stewart L. Udall, suggested that Robert Frost read a poem at the ceremony.

Frost agreed to read one of his poems, but Kennedy asked Frost if he would write something new for the ceremony. Frost didn't think he could write a poem just because someone asked him to. He said he would read his poem "The Gift Outright."

As the days passed, Frost decided he would write a new poem after all.

An Early Rejection

As a young man, Frost studied at Harvard University. When he told his teachers he wrote poetry, they did not take him seriously. One teacher teased him, saying, "So, we're a writer, are we?" Frost was angry and embarrassed. His teachers did not think his poetry was worth reading.

Inauguration Day

On a cold, windy winter day in Washington DC, Frost stepped up to the microphone. It was inauguration day, January 20, 1961, and Frost wanted to do his best to honor the new president. When he tried to read his new poem, the bright sun made it hard to see the words. He said, "I am not having a good light here at all." Vice President Lyndon B. Johnson stepped forward and tried to use his hat to shade the paper. Finally, Frost decided to skip reading the new poem. Instead, he stood tall and began "The Gift Outright" from memory. When he was finished, the audience clapped loudly for a long time.

"The Gift Outright"

The poem Robert Frost spoke aloud at the inauguration of President John F. Kennedy was "The Gift Outright." The president asked Frost to change the word "would" in the last line to "will" for the occasion. Kennedy thought the change would make the poem's ending sound more positive. Frost spoke the last line of the poem, ". . . such as she will become," referring to the future of America.

Stewart L. Udall sent a telegram to Robert Frost, asking him to read a poem at President Kennedy's inauguration. Frost replied with the following telegram the next day:

> *IF YOU CAN BEAR AT YOUR AGE THE HONOR OF BEING MADE PRESIDENT OF THE UNITED STATES, I OUGHT TO BE ABLE AT MY AGE TO BEAR THE HONOR OF TAKING SOME PART IN YOUR INAUGURATION. I MAY NOT BE EQUAL TO IT BUT I CAN ACCEPT IT FOR MY CAUSE—THE ARTS, POETRY, NOW FOR THE FIRST TIME TAKEN INTO THE AFFAIRS OF STATESMEN.*

> *Source: "Poetry and Power: Robert Frost's Inaugural Reading." Poets.org. Academy of American Poets, 2012. Web. Accessed October 26, 2012.*

What's the Big Idea?

Reread Frost's telegram. What is the main idea of Frost's reply to the invitation? Do you think he was happy to be asked to read? Why or why not? In your own words, describe why you think Frost agreed to read a poem at the inauguration.

CHAPTER TWO

A Difficult Childhood

When Robert Frost was being birthed, his father, William Prescott Frost, Jr., told the doctor that if anything went wrong, he would shoot him. Fortunately, all went well. Robert Lee Frost was born on March 26, 1874, in San Francisco, California.

At the time, Will was a newspaper reporter. He was a smart man with many talents. But he also had

The city of San Francisco, as it would have looked in the 1800s, around the time Robert Frost was born

a bad temper. Robert Frost's mother, Belle Moodie, was a teacher from Scotland. She and Will were very different from each other. She was religious, shy, and careful. Will was bold, wild, and carefree.

Living in San Francisco

San Francisco was a beautiful place to live. But Robert was growing up in an unhappy home. His father was disappointed with his job and his life, so he began to drink. When he drank, he became very angry. Robert's mother was afraid of him. To cope, she spent more time praying. During this time, Robert's sister, Jeanie, was born on June 25, 1876.

School and No School

Living with his angry father made Robert a fearful boy. When it was time for him to start school, he didn't want to go. He went for one day. He was afraid of the bus ride and the other children. He told his mother he never wanted to go to school again. Belle let him stay home. She decided she would teach Robert herself.

Although Frost struggled through school as a child, he taught at many colleges as an adult.

But the lessons did not go well. He did not want to learn to read. So Belle read to him and told him stories. Hearing the poems and stories made Robert curious about the world.

Worried about Jeanie

Robert's sister, Jeanie, was a nervous girl. She was often sick. She did not sleep well, and she was sometimes very depressed. Jeanie would try to attend school, but then she would have to quit because she would have problems. Robert worried about her. He was also worried about himself. He also struggled with depression and fear. When he would begin to feel sad, he would try to make himself feel better by working harder.

Moving Back East

On May 5, 1885, when Robert was 11, his father died. He had been ill for some time. Will's death left Belle, Robert, and Jeanie with no money. Will's parents offered to take them in. The family made the long journey across the country to Lawrence, Massachusetts, by train.

Belle found a job as a teacher, and the family moved into a small apartment. Robert and Jeanie became students in Belle's classroom. Robert did very well in this school. On weekends the family would sometimes go to his aunt and uncle's farm. Here he learned to love berry picking and life on the farm.

In the fall of 1888, Robert started high school. He worked hard and earned high grades. His mother continued teaching, but she didn't make much money. The family often didn't have as much as they needed. During his senior year, Frost met a student named Elinor White. Elinor was also a good student. She and Frost competed for the highest grades.

Published

During his sophomore year of high school, Robert learned about the Aztecs' fight for freedom against the Spaniards. He wrote a poem about it called "La Noche Triste." He gave the poem to his high school newspaper, the *Bulletin*. The poem was published in the April 1890 issue. A month later Robert submitted another poem, "Song of the Wave," and it also appeared in print. With the publication of these two poems, Robert began to think of himself as a poet.

CHAPTER THREE

Love and Family

Robert Frost was in love with Elinor White. Elinor felt the same way about him. They both adored poetry and enjoyed taking long walks in the countryside. After they graduated from high school, Frost wanted to get married right away. Elinor thought they could wait to marry. She wanted to further her education.

Frost attended Dartmouth College in New Hampshire while Elinor studied at St. Lawrence University in New York.

Both Frost and Elinor went to college. Frost attended Dartmouth College in New Hampshire. Elinor went to St. Lawrence University in New York. Frost soon decided he did not like college. He felt he was more curious about learning than the other students at his school. He wanted to be around people who loved learning and who wanted to talk about ideas. He was also missing Elinor.

At the time, Frost's mother was still teaching. Some of the older boys in her class were misbehaving, so Frost used this as an excuse to leave Dartmouth. He moved to his mother's town to help her teach.

Writing Poetry

Frost felt restless and unsure of his direction in life. He began to read Shakespeare. He studied the rhythm of the words because he wanted to use a similar rhythm in his own poetry. One night Frost sat down and wrote a poem. He called it "My Butterfly: An Elegy." When he finished and reread the poem, he cried with joy. He had finally created something truly beautiful.

Frost sent the poem to a magazine called the *Independent*. They agreed to publish it.

Elinor graduated from college in June 1895. On December 19, 1895, Elinor and Frost were married. Shortly before this, Frost's mother opened her own school. Now Elinor and Frost moved in with Belle and Jeanie, and all four taught at the school. Frost continued to write poems.

A Son Is Born

Soon Elinor became pregnant. On September 25, 1896, she gave birth to a son. They named him Elliott. Elinor was happy to be a mother. She devoted herself to raising the little boy.

"My Butterfly: An Elegy"

Robert Frost was paid $15 for the publication of "My Butterfly: An Elegy." This was the first time he had ever been paid for his writing. The poem was inspired by a butterfly wing he saw on the ground while walking outside. An elegy is a poem written in memory of someone who has died.

Frost attended Harvard University after the birth of Elliott in hopes of earning more money for his family.

Frost was still feeling uneasy. The teaching job did not make enough money to support his family. He worried so much he felt sick. He decided to go back to college. If he got a teaching degree, he could make more money for his family. He thought he might like teaching high school.

Back to School

Frost enrolled at Harvard University, and his grandfather agreed to pay his tuition. He studied the classics at Harvard, including Latin and Greek. He did very well in his studies, and he especially liked reading epic verse. Frost focused on the rhythm of the words. He believed the important thing about poetry was the way it sounded when spoken aloud.

Frost loved learning, but he felt a great deal of stress. His mother wasn't well. Elinor was pregnant with their second child. He found a part-time job to help pay rent and buy food. All these things made him tired, and soon he was having health problems. Frost decided to leave

"The Hardship of Accounting"

Frost's grandfather gave him five dollars a week to buy things he needed while he was at Dartmouth. His grandfather wanted Frost to keep a record of how he used every penny he spent. Frost did not like this. All through his life he never liked to worry about money. In the 1930s he wrote a poem called "The Hardship of Accounting." The poem expresses Frost's opinion that people shouldn't have to keep track of how they spend their money.

Harvard. On April 28, 1899, his daughter Lesley was born.

Frost saw a doctor. The doctor said he needed to change his way of life. He needed to spend time outdoors and get away from the stress of teaching. The family rented a small house on a little farm. They began to raise chickens. Frost had finally found something he loved to do. He built chicken coops and took on the life of a farmer.

Losing Elliott

During this time, Belle came to live with the Frost family. She was dying of cancer but loved to spend time with Elliott, who was three years old. In July 1900 Elliott got sick. Robert and Elinor didn't realize just how sick he was. By the time they called the doctor, nothing could be done to save him, and Elliott died.

Frost and his wife were heartbroken. For days Elinor didn't speak. Frost thought it was his fault for not calling the doctor in time. Their grief pulled them away from each other.

A young Frost, photographed around 1910

The stress of Elliott's death made Frost's health problems worse. He had pains in his chest. He had nightmares and would sweat heavily. Frost's mother was becoming more ill as well. There was no money to pay rent. It seemed as if everything was going wrong.

CHAPTER FOUR

The Poet Farmer

Elinor's mother wanted to help the Frosts. She suggested they look at a farm that was for sale on the road to Derry, New Hampshire.

The Frosts loved it. Grandfather Frost said he would buy the farm for them. After they moved to the farm, Frost's mother died. Frost felt terrible. He thought he should have done more for her. He became very depressed and wasn't able to work or

The Frost family lived on this farm in Derry, New Hampshire, from 1900 through 1911.

Time with the Family

Frost was a hands-on father. Instead of sending his children to school in town, Frost and Elinor taught them at home. Their days were spent tending the animals, growing and harvesting food, learning, and playing. Frost and Elinor passed on their love of books, words, and poetry. Frost encouraged his children to memorize many poems.

write. Elinor struggled to do the farm work by herself.

Nature Heals

As spring came, Frost's mood lightened. He began working on the farm. He took one-year-old Lesley to see the changes spring brings. The house sat between rolling hills and ridges with pretty views all around. There were raspberries, blackberries, and cranberries for picking. Slowly Frost began to enjoy life again.

Soon he had more reasons to be happy. Within a few years, he had three more children. His son, Carol, was born on May 27, 1902. On June 27, 1903, another daughter, Irma, was born. Then Marjorie was born on March 29, 1905.

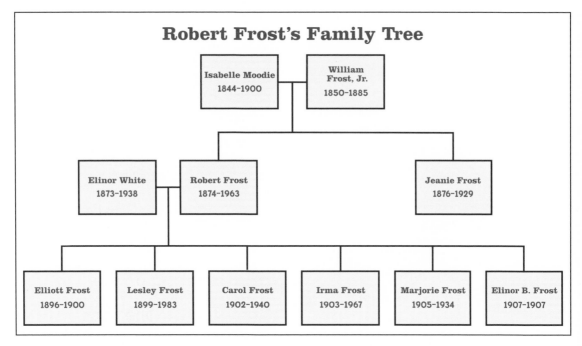

Robert Frost's Family Tree

Robert Frost's Family Tree

Take a look at Robert Frost's family tree. What information can you gather about Frost's family from this chart?

Farming, Teaching, and Poetry

The Frosts lived on the Derry farm for more than ten years. At the Derry farm, Frost would often write poems after his wife and children were asleep.

With four small children to raise, money was always tight for the Frosts. In 1906 Frost found a teaching job at Pinkerton Academy, only two miles (3 km) from his farm. He taught English to high school students. He loved teaching, but the demands of the

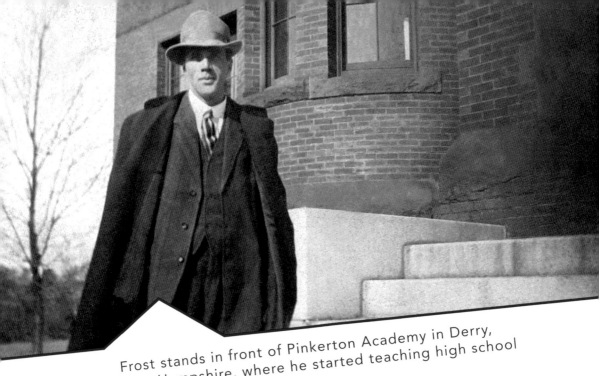

Frost stands in front of Pinkerton Academy in Derry, New Hampshire, where he started teaching high school English in 1906.

FURTHER EVIDENCE

There is quite a bit of information about Robert Frost in Chapter Four. It covers Frost's life as a farmer and writer in New Hampshire. If you could pick out the main point of the chapter, what would it be? What evidence is given to support that point? Visit the Web site below to learn more about Frost. Choose a quote from the Web site and write a few sentences explaining how it relates to this chapter.

Robert Frost Farm
www.robertfrostfarm.org/history.html

job caused him to get sick again. Frost missed two months of work to recover from pneumonia.

Elinor was also doing poorly. She was pregnant with their sixth child, Elinor Bettina. The baby was sickly and died soon after her birth on June 18, 1907. The Frosts realized they couldn't take care of everything at the farm while Frost was teaching. The family decided to move to the nearby town of Derry Village. Then Frost got a job teaching in Plymouth, New Hampshire, and the family moved there. During this time, Frost continued to write poetry, and a few of his poems were published in magazines.

An Unusual Teacher

While teaching at Plymouth Normal School, Frost became known for his unusual teaching methods. He didn't give long speeches. He liked to read to his students or just talk with them. One of his students remembered his "original approach to teaching, with a sharp wit and headstrong manner that was so different from any of the other teachers."

CHAPTER FIVE

Published in England

In 1912 Frost was 38 years old. He was having a hard time teaching and writing poetry. His dream was to publish a book of his poems. Frost decided to stop teaching and work only on his poetry. The Frosts decided to move to England. Frost would focus on his writing, and the family would have an adventure. They packed up and sailed for England on a steamship.

This portrait of Robert Frost was taken between 1910 and 1920, around the time he and his family moved to England.

A Boy's Will

The family settled into a small cottage in Beaconsfield, about 21 miles (34 km) from London. The Frosts taught the children at home and spent time on long nature walks. Without the stress of teaching, Frost was able to focus on his poetry.

Soon Frost made a collection of his earlier poems. In 1913 a small publishing house, David Nutt and Company, agreed to publish his poems as a book. Frost chose the book's title, *A Boy's Will*, from a poem by Henry Wadsworth Longfellow, one of his favorite poets. Finally the world would be able to read a collection of Frost's poems.

Ezra Pound, also an American poet, wrote a review about Frost's work *A Boy's Will*.

The first reviews of *A Boy's Will* were not great. American writer Ezra Pound's review appeared in the May 1913 issue of *Poetry: A Magazine of Verse*. Frost was upset that Pound called his poetry "simple and untutored." As time went on, however, the book received better reviews. Still Frost was not completely happy. His wife's health was poor, and the whole family was homesick. The family was longing to live in the country again, so they rented a little cottage. Frost began to feel guilty. He thought his career as a poet was hurting the people he loved most.

North of Boston

Frost worked hard to put together poems for his second book. On May 15, 1914, Frost's second book of poems, *North of Boston*, was published. Some people think this is his best book ever. He became quite well known. Many people stopped by the cottage to visit the famous poet.

Back to America

England declared war on Germany on August 4, 1914. Soon life began to change for the Frosts. Friends were going off to war, and travel became difficult. The children were homesick for America. As the war raged on, the Frosts worried they might not be able to leave England if they remained much longer. It was a hard choice, but the Frosts decided to sail back to the United States.

In 1915 the Henry Holt Publishing Company in New York began printing and selling the books Frost had published in England. Now Frost was famous in his own country as well.

Robert and Elinor Frost photographed with their children around 1910

EXPLORE ONLINE

The focus of Chapter Five is Frost's literary career. It also discusses his time in England. The Robert Frost Web site focuses on the same subjects. How is the information on the Web site different from the information in this chapter? What information is the same? How do the two sources present similar information in different ways? What can you learn from this Web site?

Modern American Poetry: Robert Frost's Life and Career
www.english.illinois.edu/maps/poets/a_f/frost/life.htm

CHAPTER SIX

Joys and Sorrows

The Frosts bought another small farm in Franconia, New Hampshire. In November 1916 Frost published his third book of poems, *Mountain Interval*. He was invited to teach at the college in Amherst, Massachusetts. The family moved to Amherst, but once again Frost found that teaching left him no time to write.

The Frost's mailbox outside the farm the family occupied in Franconia, New Hampshire, from 1915 to 1920

Many Moves

In March 1920 the family moved back to the farm in Franconia. Frost was now famous, and people came to his little farm to meet him. Soon the Frosts decided to move again. The family chose an old stone and wood house in South Shaftsbury, Vermont. Frost continued to speak at colleges and write. In June 1921 Frost started teaching at the University of Michigan in Ann Arbor, but he returned home to Vermont in June 1922. It was there that he wrote one of his most famous poems, "Stopping by Woods on a Snowy Evening."

Illness and Loss

Over the years between 1922 and 1938, Frost suffered the illnesses and deaths of his sister Jeanie and his daughter Marjorie. The hardest one to take was the death of his dear wife, Elinor. Early in 1938 Elinor had a series of heart attacks that eventually took her life. Frost was heartbroken. He moved into an apartment in Boston and bought a black and white border collie named Gillie to help ease his loneliness.

1900	Frost family moves to the farm in Derry	**Farming**
1906	Teaches at Pinkerton Academy in Derry, New Hampshire	**Teaching**
1911	Teaches at New Hampshire State Normal School	
1912	Frost family moves to England; lives in small cottage in Beaconsfield	
1914	Family moves to another country home in England called Little Iddens	
1915	Family moves to farm in Franconia, New Hampshire	
1917	Teaches at Amherst College	
1920	Family moves to the Stone House in the country, Shaftsbury, Vermont	
1921	Teaches at University of Michigan and begins first of 42 summers lecturing at the Bread Loaf School of English at Middlebury College, Ripton, Vermont	
1923	Teaches at Amherst College	
1925	Teaches at University of Michigan	
1926	Teaches at Amherst College	
1928	Buys farm, "The Gulley," in Shaftsbury, Vermont	
1933	Teaches at Pierson College, Yale University	
1939	Teaches at Harvard University / Buys farm in Ripton, Vermont, for summers	
1943	Teaches at Dartmouth College	
1949	Teaches at Amherst College	

Frost's Life of Teaching and Farming, 1900–1949

Frost was a restless man. He loved teaching, but he found that when he was teaching, he didn't have enough energy left for writing poetry. So he would teach for a while and then move to the country again. Being in nature inspired his poetry. Look at this chart. It shows some of the many changes in Frost's life. Compare it with the information in the text. How is it the same? How is it different?

Robert Frost's beloved dog Gillie was Frost's constant companion and friend for many years.

Final Years

After his wife Elinor's death in 1938, Frost moved to Boston. Feeling cramped in his small apartment, Frost bought a farm in Ripton, Vermont. He spent his time writing poetry, reading, and hiking in the countryside.

In 1943 Frost returned to Dartmouth College to work. He stayed until 1949. His last book, *In the Clearing*, was published when he was 88 years old, and it became a best seller.

Frost died in his sleep on January 29, 1963. His life was not easy, but he used his sorrow and joys to create poetry that lives on for all of us to enjoy.

"The Road Not Taken"

Two roads diverged in a yellow wood,
And sorry I could not travel both
And be one traveler, long I stood
And looked down one as far as I could
To where it bent in the undergrowth;

Then took the other, as just as fair,
And having perhaps the better claim,
Because it was grassy and wanted wear;
Though as for that the passing there
Had worn them really about the same,

And both that morning equally lay
In leaves no step had trodden black.
Oh, I kept the first for another day!
Yet knowing how way leads on to way,
I doubted if I should ever come back.

I shall be telling this with a sigh
Somewhere ages and ages hence:
Two roads diverged in a wood, and I—

I took the one less traveled by,
And that has made all the difference.

Source: Robert Frost. Mountain Interval. *New York: Henry Holt, 1916. Print. 9.*

What's the Big Idea?

What is the main idea of Frost's poem? Choose two or three details and explain how they support the main idea.

IMPORTANT DATES

1874
Robert Lee Frost is born in San Francisco, California, on March 26.

1890
Frost writes his first poem, "La Noche Triste."

1895
Frost marries Elinor White on December 19.

1906
Frost begins teaching at Pinkerton Academy.

1913
Frost's first book, *A Boy's Will*, is published in England in April.

1914
On May 15 Frost's second book, *North of Boston*, is published in England.

1915
Frost begins giving readings and talks. Henry Holt and Company publishes his book *North of Boston* in the United States.

1938
Elinor dies of a heart attack.

1963
Robert Frost dies in his sleep on January 29.

KEY WORKS

A Boy's Will

This was Frost's first published book of poetry. It was first published in England by David Nutt and Co. Later Henry Holt & Co. published this book in the United States.

Frost, Robert. *A Boy's Will.* New York: Henry Holt, 1915.

Collected Poems

Frost won his second Pulitzer Prize for this collection of poems. It includes poems from all of his previous books.

Frost, Robert. *Collected Poems.* New York: Henry Holt, 1930.

A Further Range

Some people complained the poems in this book were too political, but it won the Pulitzer Prize.

Frost, Robert. *A Further Range.* New York: Henry Holt, 1936.

New Hampshire

New Hampshire is the first of Frost's books to win the Pulitzer Prize. It includes "Stopping by Woods on a Snowy Evening," one of his most famous poems. He wrote the entire poem one morning in June 1922.

Frost, Robert. *New Hampshire*, New York: Henry Holt, 1923.

North of Boston

Many claim this is Frost's best collection of poems. It became a best seller and includes favorite poems like "Mending Wall" and "After Apple-Picking." This was the first of Frost's books to be published in the United States.

Frost, Robert. *North of Boston*, New York: Henry Holt, 1914.

A Witness Tree

Frost won his fourth and final Pulitzer for this book. It contains the poem "The Gift Outright," which Frost recited at John F. Kennedy's inauguration ceremony.

Frost, Robert. *A Witness Tree.* New York: Henry Holt, 1942.

Another View

Find another source about Frost's life and work. Write a short essay comparing and contrasting the point of view of your source with the point of view of this book's author. Be sure to answer these questions: What is the point of view of each author? How are they similar? How are they different?

Take a Stand

When Frost first began to write poetry, many readers did not take him seriously. Read through the poem included in this book and search more of his poetry online. Why do you think people may have not liked his poetry? What do you think of Frost's poetry? Do you like it? Why or why not? Take a position about his poetry and write a short essay describing your opinion. Give reasons for your opinion and facts and details to support your reasons.

You Are There

Imagine that you are one of Frost's children, living on the farm in Derry. Write 300 words describing your days on the farm. What do you and your siblings do each day? What is it like to have Robert Frost for a father? What do you like or dislike about your life?

Why Do I Care?

Think about Robert Frost's life story. Have you ever felt restless or frustrated? Have you ever tried to create something, like a poem? Think about two or three ways Frost's story connects with your own life. Write about the connections you discover.

GLOSSARY

classics
famous writings from the past

declare
to openly announce
something

depressed
feeling sad and hopeless

devoted
gave time and attention

grief
deep sadness

hands-on
active and involved

inauguration
a ceremony that starts a
president's term in office

literary
related to reading and writing

opinion
one's own thoughts and
beliefs

original
one's very own creative
thoughts or actions

published
printed in books or
magazines for anyone to read

reviews
writings giving an opinion
about whether something
was good or not

LEARN MORE

Books

Frost, Robert. *You Come Too: Favorite Poems for All Ages.* New York: Henry Holt, 2002.

Frost, Robert, and Grandma Moses. *A Prayer in Spring.* New York: Universe Publishing, 2011.

Schmidt, Gary D., ed. *Poetry for Young People: Robert Frost.* New York: Sterling, 2008.

Web Links

To learn more about Robert Frost, visit ABDO Publishing Company online at **www.abdopublishing.com.** Web sites about Robert Frost are featured on our Book Links page. These links are routinely monitored and updated to provide the most current information available.

Visit **www.mycorelibrary.com** for free additional tools for teachers and students.

INDEX

Boy's Will, A, 32–33
Bulletin, 15

Dartmouth College, 18, 21, 39, 40

Frost, Carol, 26, 27
Frost, Elinor Bettina, 27, 29
Frost, Elinor White, 15, 17–21, 22, 26, 27, 29, 38
Frost, Elliott, 19, 22, 27
Frost, Irma, 26, 27
Frost, Jeanie, 12, 14, 19, 27, 38
Frost, Lesley, 22, 26, 27
Frost, Marjorie, 26, 27, 38
Frost, William Prescott, Jr., 11–12, 14, 27

"Gift Outright, The," 7, 8

Harvard University, 7, 20–22, 39

Johnson, Lyndon B., 8

Kennedy, John F., 7, 8, 9

"La Noche Triste," 15
Longfellow, Henry Wadsworth, 32

Moodie, Belle, 12–13, 14–15, 19, 22, 25, 27
Mountain Interval, 37
"My Butterfly: An Elegy," 18, 19

North of Boston, 34

Pinkerton Academy, 27, 39
Plymouth Normal School, 29
Poetry: A Magazine of Verse, 33
Pound, Ezra, 32, 33

"Road Not Taken, The," 32, 41

"Song of the Wave," 15
"Stopping by Woods on a Snowy Evening," 38

Thomas, Edward, 32

Yeats, William Butler, 32

ABOUT THE AUTHOR

Susan Temple Kesselring is a kindergarten to first grade teacher, children's book writer, and mother of five daughters. She lives in Minnesota with her husband, Rob, and crazy dog, Lois Lane. She loves kids, books, music, and nature.